Presidents' Day

by Helen Frost

Consulting Editor: Gail Saunders-Smith, Ph.D.
Consultant: Alexa Sandmann, Ed.D.
Professor of Literacy
The University of Toledo
Member, National Council for the Social Studies

Pebble Books

an imprint of Capstone Press
Mankato, Minnesota

Pebble Books are published by Capstone Press
151 Good Counsel Drive, P.O. Box 669, Mankato, Minnesota 56002
www.capstonepress.com

Printed in the United States of America in North Mankato, MN
072011   006231CGVMI

Library of Congress Cataloging-in-Publication Data
Frost, Helen, 1949–
    Presidents' Day/by Helen Frost.
    p.cm.—(National holidays)
    Includes bibliographical references and index.
    Summary: Simple text and photographs explain Presidents' Day and why we
celebrate it to honor those who have been president.
    ISBN-13: 978-0-7368-0545-2 (hardcover)
    ISBN-10: 0-7368-0545-1 (hardcover)
    ISBN-13: 978-0-7368-8729-8 (softcover pbk.)
    ISBN-10: 0-7368-8729-6 (softcover pbk.)
    1. Presidents' Day—Juvenile literature. 2. Presidents—United States—History—
Juvenile literature. [1. Presidents' Day. 2. Presidents. 3. Holidays.] I. Title. II. Series.
E176.8.F76   2000
394.261   99-049613

Note to Parents and Teachers

The National Holidays series supports national social studies standards related to understanding events that celebrate the values and principles of American democracy. This book describes and illustrates Presidents' Day. The photographs support early readers in understanding the text. This book also introduces early readers to subject-specific vocabulary words, which are defined in the Words to Know section. Early readers may need assistance to read some words and to use the Table of Contents, Words to Know, Read More, Internet Sites, and Index/Word List sections of the book.

Table of Contents

Presidents' Day is a day
to honor U.S. presidents.

6

Presidents' Day became
a national holiday in
1968. Americans celebrate
Presidents' Day every year
on the third Monday
of February.

Two of the most famous
presidents were born
in February. George
Washington was born
on February 22, 1732.
Abraham Lincoln was born
on February 12, 1809.

George Washington was an army general during the Revolutionary War (1775–1783). Americans elected George the first U.S. president in 1789.

Abraham Lincoln was president during the Civil War (1861–1865). People remember Abraham for keeping the United States together.

Presidents' Day is a day to honor all U.S. presidents. Every president works to make the United States better.

Some people visit memorials to presidents on Presidents' Day. They remember what U.S. presidents have done.

HOURS
LOBBY
Mon.-Thurs.   9:00AM - 4:30PM
Friday   9:00AM - 6:00PM
DRIVE UP
Mon.-Thurs.   8:00AM - 5:30PM
Friday   8:00AM - 6:00PM
Saturday   8:30AM -12:00PM

Closed for
Presidents' Day

Some people close their businesses to honor Presidents' Day. Many banks, schools, and government offices are closed on Presidents' Day.

People read about the presidents on Presidents' Day. Some people think about becoming president.

Words to Know

Civil War—the U.S. war between the Northern states and the Southern states; the Civil War was fought from 1861 to 1865.

honor—to show respect; Americans honor U.S. presidents on Presidents' Day.

national—having to do with a nation as a whole; Presidents' Day is a holiday for the whole country.

president—the elected leader of a country; U.S. citizens elect a president every four years.

Revolutionary War—the war in which the 13 American colonies won their independence from Great Britain; the Revolutionary War was fought from 1775 to 1783.

Read More

Ansary, Mir Tamim. *Presidents' Day.* Holiday Histories. Des Plaines, Ill.: Heinemann Library, 1999.

Margaret, Amy. *Presidents' Day.* Library of Holidays. New York: PowerKids Press, 2002.

Nelson, Robin. *Presidents' Day.* First Step Nonfiction. Minneapolis: Lerner, 2003.

Schaefer, Lola M. *George Washington.* Famous Americans. Mankato, Minn.: Pebble Books, 1999.

Internet Sites

FactHound offers a safe, fun way to find Internet sites related to this book.

Go to *www.facthound.com*

He'll fetch the best sites for you!

FactHound will fetch the best sites for you!

Index/Word List

Word Count: 164
Early-Intervention Level: 18

Editorial Credits
Mari C. Schuh, editor; Heather Kindseth, cover designer; Linda Clavel, illustrator; Kimberly Danger, photo researcher

Photo Credits
Archive Photos, 10; Archive Photos/Lambert, 8 (left)
Arnie Sachs/CNP/Archive Photos, 14
Arthur Tilley/FPG International LLC, 4
David F. Clobes, 6, 18, 20
Hirz/Archive Photos, 12
Library of Congress, 8 (right)
Mark Reinstein/FPG International LLC, 1
Unicorn Stock Photos/M. Finefrock, 16